PYTHON FOR
DATA ANALYSIS:

Improve Your Skills With The Complete
Beginner's Guide For Coding With
Python For Data Analysis.

TABLE OF CONTENTS

INTRODUCTION

The following chapters will discuss all of the things that we need to know when it is time to work on our own data analysis for the first time. Many companies have heard about data analysis and are curious to know how this works and what they can do with it. However, many are not sure the right steps to take to see the best results. This guidebook is not only going to walk you through completing your own data analysis but will ensure that you are set and able to do it all with the Python coding language as well.

This guidebook is going to look at some of the basics that you need to do to start with your own data analysis. This is going to ensure that you are set to start this process on your own and that you will see some of the results of better decision making, cutting down waste, beating out the competition, and reaching your customers better than ever before. To start with this process, we spent a bit of time learning more about the data analysis and what this is all about. There are some steps that we need to know about to get started with this process, and we will talk about the basics of data analysis, some of the benefits of working with this process, and the steps or the lifecycle that works with our data analysis as well.

There are a ton of benefits that show up when we talk about the Python data analysis and any industry, and any business will be able to benefit when they choose to use this for their own needs as well. When you are ready to learn some more about the Python language and how it can work to improve your data analytic skills to help your business, make sure to check out this guidebook to help you get started.

Given the nature of competition in the business world, it is not easy to keep customers happy. Competitors keep preying on each other's customers, and those who win have another challenge ahead, how to maintain the customers lest they slide back to their former business partners? This is one area where Data Analysis comes in handy.

To understand their customers better, companies rely on data. They collect all manner of data at each point of interaction with their customers. Data are useful in several ways. The companies learn more about their customers, after that, clustering them according to their specific needs. Through such segmentation, the company can attend to the customers' needs better and hope to keep them satisfied for longer.

There is so much more to Data Analysis than corporate and government decisions. As a programmer, you are venturing into an industry that is challenging and exciting at the same time. Data doesn't lie unless it is manipulated, in which case you need insane Data Analysis and handling skills. As a data analyst, you will come across many challenges and problems that need solutions that can only be handled through Data Analysis. The way you interact with data can make a huge difference, more significant than you can imagine.

As you interact with data, you do understand the importance of cleaning data to ensure the outcome of your analysis is not flawed. You will learn how to go about this and build on that to make sure your work is perfect. Another challenge that many organizations have is protecting the integrity of data. You should try to protect your organization from using contaminated data. There are procedures you can put in place to make sure that you use clean data all the time.

CHAPTER 1:

WHAT IS DATA ANALYSIS

What is Data Analysis?

When it comes to working with data analysis, there are going to be a few methods that you can work with. These phases will ensure that you can handle the data correctly and that it will work the way that we want it to. These are going to include some of the initial phases of cleaning our data, working with whether the data is high enough quality, quality measurement analysis, and then we enter into the main data analysis.

All of these steps are going to be relevant to the work that we want to do with data analysis. Without all of them, even though some may seem to have nothing to do with data analysis in the first place, our analysis is not going to be very accurate or useful. Since companies are often going to rely on these analyses for important decisions, having accurate and high-quality data is going to be necessary.

The first step that we need to focus on here is data cleaning. This is the first process, and while it may not be as much fun as we see with the algorithms and more that come with data analysis, they are still important. This is the part of the process where we match up records, check for multiples and duplicates in the data, and get rid of anything that is false or does not match up with what we are looking for at this time.

When that part is done with the part of cleaning our data, it is time for us to go through and do a bit of quality assurance here. We want to make sure that the data we work with is going to work for any algorithm that we would like to focus our time and attention on. Using things like frequency counts and descriptive statistics can help us out with this.

It is never a good idea to go through and analyze data that does not meet some of your own personal standards. You want to make sure that it will match up with what you want to do with some of your work on the analysis, that it is accurate, and it will get the job done for you, as well.

When the quality analysis part is done, it is time to make sure that the measurement tools that we use here are going to be higher in quality as well. If you are not using the same measurements on each part of this, then your results will be skewed in the process. If you are using the right ones, though, you will find that this gives you some options that are more accurate and can help you really rely on the data analysis.

Once the whole process of making sure you clean the data, and we have done the quality analysis and the measurement, it is time to dive into the analysis that we want to use. There are a ton of different analysis that we can do on the information, and it often will depend on what your goals are in this whole process. We can go through and do some graphical techniques that include scattering plots. We can work with some frequency counts to see what percentages and numbers are present. We can do some continuous variables or even the computation of new variables.

There are tons of algorithms that are present when we work on this, and it will again depend on your goals. Some are better for helping you to see the best decision to make out of several options, such as the decision tree and random forest.

The Main Data Analysis

Now it is time for us to go through and work with what is known as the main data analysis. Many parts come with this as well, and we have to remember that this is a significant process. It will take some time and is not always as easy and straightforward as we would hope in the beginning. During this part, after we have had a chance to go through and clean the data and get it organized, including cleaning it off and some of the work that we did before, it is time to enter into the main data analysis to get some things done in the manner that we want.

There are a few methods that we need to use to make this work. For example, the affirmative and exploratory approaches will help us out. These are not going to allow us to have a clear hypothesis stated before we analyze the data. This ensures that we are not going to be tempted to bring in our ideas to the mix. We will go through the information and see what is there, and I hope that be able to learn something from it in the process.

Then we can check on some of the stability that shows up in the results. The stability of the results using cross-validation, statistical methods, and sensitivity analysis is going to help. We want to make sure that the results we can get are accurate and will be able to repeat themselves. If we run through it a few times and end up with a few different answers, how are we supposed to know which result is the right one for us? This takes some time and dedication to be done but can be the right method to help us out.

We can then work with a few different methods of statistics to help us pick out the algorithm that we want to work with and to make sure that we can see what is going on with everything. Some of the statistical methods that we can utilize here will include:

The general linear model: There are many models of statistics that are going to work with the general linear model to get things done. This is going to help us to work with some of the dependent variables that are there, and we can even work with what is known as a multiple linear regression if there are several of these dependent variables as well.

Generalized linear model: This is similar to the other option that we talked about, but it is often considered as more of a generalization or the extension of that model. It is used to help with some of the discrete dependent variables that are out there.

Item response theory. The models that are used for this one are going to spend time assessing one latent variable from some of the other binary measured variables that are out there.

In addition to this, there are tons of different approaches that you can use to analyze your data. They can all be fun, and in some cases, you will be able to utilize more than one of these at a time. It all depends on what you want to do with the data. A few of the options that are available to try out include:

A cross-cultural analysis to see if the same results are going to happen between different countries or different cultures.

- Content analysis

- The grounded theory analysis

- The discourse analysis

- The narrative analysis

- The hermeneutic analysis

- The ethnographic analysis.

Keep in mind that when we are doing some of the data analysis work that we want to accomplish, a lot of it is going to have nothing to do with the actual analysis that we want to use. There will be a good deal of time spent on understanding the data at hand and cleaning it off. Also, we even need to take care in picking out the right algorithm that we want to use.

That does not mean that the analysis is not important. However, for the analysis to truly work, we need to make sure that all of those other parts are in place and working well too. This ensures that we have high-quality data that can train our machine learning algorithms well and provide us with some of the results that we want in the process. When we take our time and really do the previous steps properly, we know with certainty that the results and insights that we get from the actual data analysis will be accurate and can work for our needs as well.

Data Science vs. Data Analysis

The terms of data science and data analytics are often used interchangeably. However, these terms are entirely different and have different implications for different businesses. Data science encompasses a variety of scientific models and methods that can be used to manipulate and analyze structured, semi-structured, and unstructured data. Tools and processes that can be used to gain insight from highly complex, unorganized, and raw data set come under the umbrella of data science. Unlike data analytics that is targeted to verify a hypothesis, data science boils down to connecting data points to identify new patterns and insights that can be made use of in future planning for the business. Data science moves the business from inquiry to insights by providing a new perspective into their structured and unstructured data by identifying patterns that can allow businesses to increase efficiencies, reduce costs and recognize the new market opportunities.

Data science acts as a multidisciplinary blend of technology, machine learning algorithm development, statistical analysis, and data inference that provides businesses with enhanced capability to solve their most complex business problems. Data analytics falls under the umbrella of data science and pertains more to reviewing and analyzing historical data to put it in context. Unlike data science, data analytics is characterized by low usage of artificial intelligence, predictive modeling, and machine learning algorithms to gather insights from processed and structured data using standard SQL query commands. The seemingly nuanced differences between data analytics and data science can actually have a substantial impact on an organization.

CHAPTER 2:

THE BASIC OF THE PYTHON LANGUAGE

Python — A Programming Language

Many professional programmers say that Python is one of the easiest programming languages to learn. Unlike other programming languages, you do not need to remember a lot of complicated stuff in Python.

But what exactly is a programming language anyway? As mentioned before, you need to create a program using programming languages. As a language, Python has its own words and grammar rules. The rules and words it has do not differ much with the rules and words of other programming languages. It even shares some terms with the English language.

For example, if you want your program to display a message like, "Hello World," you need to type and execute this line on Python: *print ("Hello World")*

That is how simple programming languages are. If you were to instruct your computer using the English language, you might have said this instead.

Print the sentence "Hello World" on the screen.

If you compare the two, it seems that when using a programming language to give instructions to the computer, you need to speak robotically. In a programming language, one statement or one line of command only requires a verb (action or command) and an object (receiver of the action or object of the action). Sometimes, all you need to type is a single command keyword.

It might sound simple, but there are some quirky parts that you must know. Just like human language, programming languages also follow grammar rules or syntax. Unfortunately, syntax rules of programming languages are strict. If you make a mistake, expect that the computer will not be able to follow your instruction. It might return an error or even crash if it tries to read and execute a line with incorrect syntax.

For example, if you reverse the position of the elements of the print statement mentioned a while ago, this would happen: >>> *("Hello World") print*

File "<stdin>", line 1

("Hello World") print

SyntaxError: invalid syntax

>>>

Python's syntax rules will be discussed later. For now, it is time for you to prepare the things that you need.

Prep Yourself

Thanks to the previous chapter, you may now have a decent idea about what computer programming is and how everything relates to each other. Now, for programming, you are required to have a basic knowledge of logic, abstract algebra, and college algebra.

In programming, you need to compare values most of the time, and occasionally, you might need to do it arithmetically and/or logically. Alternatively, you must have some basic knowledge about sets.

On the other hand, you must make sure that your program's flow is logical and will always lead to the result that you want. If ever there is an undesirable result, you must have a presence of mind and plan how to prevent that from happening or devise a process for how your program will handle it.

Do not worry about those things too much. Even if you do not have those traits or knowledge yet, you can always learn them. Also, if you are passionate about programming, you will learn to develop these traits as you study and create programs.

Your Tools and Wares

Once you're prepared for programming, what is next? You need to prepare your 'programming kit'. Of course, the number one requirement for programming is a computer. Ideally, a typical computer running on Microsoft Windows is enough for your programming needs.

Computer

Take note that you do not need a high-end computer for programming, especially if you are just starting. Most of the programs that you will develop will probably be limited to using small chunks of resources of your computer or device.

Truth be told, it is an advantage to use 'weak' computers for programming. Using a slow computer will make you warier about the performance of your program. If ever your program has some inefficient codes in it, you will immediately feel the performance degradation it will cause. And that will lead to an immediate awareness of the inefficient coding of your program.

Operating System

When it comes to operating systems, it is not necessary to use Microsoft Windows. Python code will work on almost any operating system environment. If you have a computer running on Mac OS or a Linux distro, then use it.

Python

Of course, you will need Python. As of this writing, the latest version of Python is Python 3.4.3. To get Python, you must go to https://www.python.org/downloads/.

In the download page, you have two primary choices of Python versions. The first one is 3.4.3, which is a stable release. And the second one is 2.7.9, which is the stable legacy version of Python.

What is the difference between the two? Well, Python version 2.7.9 is the older, more stable release of Python. Python has reached tremendous popularity with its versions 2.x.x. And due to that, most Python programmers have developed their programs under this version. As of now, most of the examples and programs made with Python use Python version 2.x.x.

Unfortunately, Python version 2.x.x is not perfect. It has its own problems. And it is said that fixing those problems and incompatibilities will require a lot of work. Also, adding functionalities has become a problem, too. Because of these reasons, Python version 3.x.x was born.

Python 3.x.x experienced major changes when it comes to syntax and performance. Unluckily, it is not that backward compatible with programs or source code made using Python 2.x.x. Nevertheless, it is possible to port those source codes in Python 3.x.x. You might need to use a third-party program. Alternatively, you might just need to rewrite the source code from scratch. And of course, you cannot fully use source code made in Python 3.x.x with Python 2.x.x.

That is just a summary of the things you need to know about the two versions. In this book, you will be taught of Python version 3.x.x.

Anyway, aside from the two versions on the page, you will see other links for other version releases of Python. If you see any version higher than the stable release, probably, it is still a beta release, and it might contain some bugs.

Installing Python

After downloading, you can simply open the installer package and let it run. An installation window will pop up, and all you need to do is to follow the steps that are indicated in the installation program.

But hold on and do not just click your way out of the installation. You will need to take note of the installation path of Python. You will need it later. On the other hand, if you are using Linux, your Linux may have Python preinstalled. However, the Python version has maybe version 2.x.x. You can check the version of Python you have in your package manager or using the terminal. On the terminal, just type: $ python --version

To get the latest version of Python, make sure that you are connected to the internet. After that, you can download and install Python using your Linux' package manager or terminal.

If you are going to use the package manager, you can just use the search function and download Python. In case you want to use the terminal, make sure that you are logged in as root or a power user. On the other hand, you can just use sudo. For example, *$ sudo apt-get install python3.4*

Source Code Editor

To create a program, you need to type your source c0de. Unfortunately, Python does not come with a source code editor. However, it does have an interactive mode or interpreter mode. Python's interpreter mode will be discussed later.

If you are on Microsoft Windows, you can just use Notepad. On the other hand, Linux distros usually have preinstalled source code editors. If you do not like the one that is in your Linux, you can try other source code editors such as Emacs, Vim, or Ed.

By the way, Notepad is not really a source code editor. It lacks the necessary features, such as syntax highlighting, for it to aid you in writing your source code. Due to that, you should get Notepad++. Notepad++ is a free source code editor that you can use instead of the simple text editor Notepad.

To understand a bit more about how Python can help us out while handling a Data Analysis, we first need to take a look at what the Python language is all about. The Python language is an object-oriented programming language (or OOP language), that is designed with the user in mind, while still providing us with the power that we need, and the extensions and libraries, that will make Data Analysis and machine learning as easy to work with as possible.

Many benefits come with the Python coding language, and this is one of the reasons why so many people like to learn how to code with this language compared to other options. First, this coding language was designed with the beginner in mind. There are a lot of coding languages that are hard to learn, and only more advanced programmers, those who have spent years in this kind of field, can learn how to use them.

This is not the case when we talk about the Python language. This one has been designed to work well for beginners. Even if you have never done any coding in Python before, you will find that this language is easy to catch on to, and you will be able to write some complex codes, even ones with enough power to handle machine learning and data science in no time at all.

Even though the Python language is an easy one to learn how to use, there is still a lot of power that comes with this language as well. This language is designed to take on some of those harder projects, the ones that may need a little extra power behind them. For example, there are a lot of extensions that come with Python that can make it work with machine learning, a process where we teach a model or a computer how to make decisions on its own.

Due to the many benefits that come with the Python coding language, many people are interested in learning more about it and how to make it work for their needs. This happens in many large communities, throughout the world, of people sharing their ideas, asking for help, and offering any advice, you may need.

This coding language also combines well with some of the other coding languages out there. While Python can do a lot of work on its own, when you combine it with some of the other libraries that are out there, sometimes it needs to be compatible with other languages as well. This is not a problem at all when it comes to Python, and you can add on any extension, and still write out the code in Python, knowing that it will be completely compatible with the library in question.

There are also a lot of different libraries that you can work with when it comes to the Python language. While we can see a lot of strong coding done with the traditional library of Python, sometimes adding some more functionality and capabilities can be the trick that is needed to get results. For example, there are many deep learning and machine learning libraries that connect with Python and can help this coding language take on some of the data science. Data Analysis projects that you want to use.

Python is also seen as an object-oriented programming language or an OOP language. This means that it is going to rely on classes and objects to help organize the information and keep things in line. The objects that we use, which are going to be based on real objects that we can find in our real world, are going to be placed in a class to pull out later when they are needed in the code. This is much easier to work with than we see with the traditional coding languages of the past and ensures that all of the different parts of your code are going to stay exactly where you would like them

As we can see here, there is so much that the Python coding language is going to be able to do to help us with our Data Analysis. There are a lot of different features and capabilities that come with Python, and this makes it perfect for almost any action or project that we want to handle. When we combine it with some of the different libraries that are available, we can get some of these more complicated tasks done.

CHAPTER 3:

The Fundamental Steps of Data Analysis

Understanding the Data Analytics Process

Now it is time for us to look a bit more into some of the mechanics that are there for useful data analysis. All of these need to be in place to ensure that the data analytics is going to work, that we get the right kind of data, and that we will be able to get all of it to flow together and do well. This is sometimes a difficult process to work with, but you will find that when we combine the parts and make sure that we understand how they work, it is easier to see what we need to do to get this done. With that in mind, let us look at the six main phases that come with data analysis and explore what we can do with each one.

The Discovery Phase

This is a fun phase to work with because it can set the stage for the rest of the project that we need to work on. This part is all about figuring out what kind of data we need, what our goals are, and what we would actually like to figure out later on after the whole analysis is done. We do not want to take this part lightly, and it usually is not a good idea to just go and gather up a bunch of data without first figuring out what we need and what we want to do.

We want to start out with a good idea of what the business wants to accomplish when they do this analysis. Do they want to figure out more about their customer base? Do they want to learn if there is a new niche, they can go into? Do they want to learn more about their competition and how they can utilize that information to get ahead? There are many reasons that companies want to use the data analysis, but if you do not have a plan in place ahead of time, then it is going to be a mess. You will waste time gathering up information, with no plan at all.

When this is done, it is time for us to figure out which methods we will use for gathering up the data. Data analysis is going to be useless if we are not able to go through and discover the data that we want to use in our algorithms. The good news is that there are tons of places with data in our modern world, and we just need to do some research and figure out which ones are going to provide us with the data that we need.

We can choose to spend some time on social media and see what people are saying to us or how they are interacting with us. We can send out surveys and do focus groups to learn a bit. We can do research online and, on some websites, to figure out what is going on there. We can look to our own websites and see what customers are buying and some of the demographics that match up there as well.

There is no limit to the amount of information that we can gather, but we want to ensure that we are gathering up the right kind of information in the process. Just because you have any data at your disposal does not mean that you are going to use it well, or that it is even relevant to what you are trying to be done. Take your time when it comes to gathering up that data and figure out what is important and what is not.

The Data Preparation Phase

Once you have had some time to prepare for the information that you want, and to figure out what questions you would like to see solved in the process, it is time for us to go through and work with the phase of data preparation. At this point, we have a bunch of data from a bunch of different places and sources. This is a great thing. However, you will not have to search through the data very long to figure out that it is a mess, and that there is some work for you to do to get it ready.

If you try to push your data through the chosen algorithm in its current state, you are not going to get accurate information and results. The algorithm will be confused at what you are trying to do along the way. There will be missing values, incomplete entries, duplicates, outliers that can throw off the average, and more. Despite the extra work that is going to happen here, your algorithms require that the data you want to be interpreted is organized and prepared properly.

There are a few things that we need to focus on to make this happen. First, we need to deal with outliers. These are going to be the points that are way far from the average and were just some once in a lifetime kind of things. If the majority of your customers are between the ages of 18 to 25, but you have a couple of customers who are 75, the older group can probably be ignored.

Those were likely individuals purchasing stuff for someone in the younger group. However, if you add them into the mix and put them through the algorithm, it is going to skew your results. You may, if you leave these outliers in there, start to think your age demographics are individuals 30 to 35 because the older group messed with things a bit and took the average too high.

Now, this does not mean that we get rid of the outliers all of the time. Many times, it does, but there are some situations where the outliers are going to tell us a lot of information in the process. If there are a decent number of outliers that fall in the same spot, this could be a goldmine, telling you of a new product or a new demographic that you could possibly reach. Maybe the average age of your customer is 18 to 25, but then you look and see there is a concentration of outliers in the 30 to 35 range. This may be something that you need to explore in more detail and then capitalize on.

In addition to working with the outliers, we need to spend some time looking at the duplicate values. Sometimes especially since we are gathering data from many different sources, we are going to end up with some information that is duplicated. This is not a big deal if it is just a few sources. However, when we have many duplicates, it is going to mess with the results that you get. It is often best to reduce and even eliminate the duplicates to get the best results.

In addition, the final thing that we need to focus on when it comes to our data preparation is to make sure that the missing values are taken care of. If you have a few missing values, then you can probably erase that part of the data and be fine. However, many times, filling it in with the mean or the average of the other columns with it can be a good way to still use that information without getting error messages from your algorithm.

Planning Out the Model Phase

Now it is time for us to move on to some model planning. This is where you and your team are going to start creating the model or the algorithms that you want to use in order to move this process along and ensure that it is going to work the way that you want. Based on the work that you did in the other two steps, the model that you choose to use is going to vary, and this is the stage where we figure out the best steps to take.

During this part, the team is going to spend some time determining which workflow, techniques, and methods are going to be needed to help us later when we build up our model. We figure out how we can best use the data that we have been collecting all this time, and work from there. The team will also need to explore some of the data they have to learn more about the relationship that is there between the variables, and then they can select the variables that are the most important here.

The reason that we are going to do this is that it helps us to figure out the models that are the most suitable to work with. When we know more about the variables, and we can find the pattern of the ones that are the most important to our needs, the model will lend itself to us pretty well. This can save us a lot of time and effort and can make sure that we do not have to work on a bunch of different models in the hopes that we will get the right one.

The Model Building Phase

The fourth phase that we are able to spend our time on is model building. This is going to be where we get to work figuring out how to make a model that can learn from the input it gets and will be able to sort through some of the data that we have as well. It is a great phase to work with and can be seen as some of the most fun as well.

In this phase, your team is going to take time to develop the sets of data that they want to use for testing, training, and for various production purposes for their algorithms as well. Also, in this phase, the team builds and then executes the models based on some of the work that has been done in the previous phase as well.

In addition, the team here is going to take the time to consider whether the tools that it already has will be enough to run the models.

Sometimes they have the right tools and more to get it all done, and other times they will need to go through and add in a more robust environment for executing their models and some of the workflows that they want to accomplish.

The Communication Phase

Once you have had a chance to work on building your model and pushing the chosen data through it, it is time for us to look at some of the key insights and patterns that are there, and communicate them to others around us. This data analysis was likely done for some reason, usually to help a company in the process, and the team who did this work must be able to help communicate this to the right people.

Sometimes, this is going to be a challenge. The individuals in the company who order this analysis may recognize the importance of doing it and want to get the results. However, they may not understand all of the technical terms like a data analyst can. It is up to you and your team to communicate the results clearly and concisely to the audience.

In this phase, the team, along with some of the major stakeholders in the company, are going to determine whether the results of the project are going to be a success or a failure based on some of the criteria that were set out in the first phase we talked about before. The team needs to be able to identify some of the key findings, quantify the business value of this, and then go through and develop a narrative to help convey and summarize the findings so everyone can understand and use them.

There are some methods that can be used to help communicate the results. You can use visuals to help show it, along with some spreadsheets and reports. Think about your audience before you get started on this one to ensure that you are presenting the data in a manner that the other party will be able to use and understand.

Operationalize

The final phase that we are going to look at here is to operationalize. This is where the team is going to take all of the work that we were able to handle and look over in the other five steps, and then deliver it to those who need it. This includes the technical documents, codes, briefings, and all of the final reports as well.

In addition, depending on the results of this, and what the suggestions and insights are all about, the company may decide to take this information and run a kind of pilot project. This allows them to implement some of the models and the other insights into a production environment and see how it is going to work. If things go well, the company may decide that it is time to take this further and try it out in other parts of the company, and their business, as well.

Each of these stages of data analytics is important. This will ensure that we can go through, organize things, and get it ready to handle some of the data using our algorithms along the way. If this process is done well, and the right care and attention are given to it all, you will find that it is easier for us to learn those insights and predictions, and we can utilize that to help us become more successful in the long-term.

CHAPTER 4:

HOW CODING WORKS

Starting to Interact with Python

O nce you have downloaded the right version of Python on your computer, you will be ready to start using it. The first thing you need to remember about the Python program is that it interacts with all of the data on your computer. The applications that you use on your PC manipulate data regardless of how simple they are. Requests on a computer will read the data on a computer, update it and then delete it once it is done. Before an application can perform this type of manipulation, it will have to be set up using a programming language like Python. Without a coding language like Python, it will nearly be impossible for a computer to understand the commands that you are making. Below are some of the things that you will need to know when attempting to work with Python.

Starting the Python Program

To start your programming experience with Python, you will have to remember a few things. The first thing that you will have to do is open the Python command line. You can find this in the Python 3.3 folder. Once you click on, it will open the command line session with the

PYTHON FOR DATA ANALYSIS:

default settings. Once it begins, you will need to type on Python and hit enter. By doing this, you will be able to open up a version of the command line that has a much higher degree of flexibility. With this option, you will be able to do things like increasing the privileges of the application you are working on. You will want to do this when trying to develop applications that use secured resources. The box that opens will usually tell you things like what version of Python is being used and how to get additional information on it.

Using the Command Line

Once you have opened the command line, you will need to start thinking about how you are going to use it to your advantage. Here are some of the things that you will be able to do with the command line. Using the options or command-line switch in the line is easy. All you will need to do is to put in a minus sign followed by a series of the letter. If you are looking to get help with the Python program, you can do so by typing in python-h and then pressing the enter button. Once you hit enter, you will be able to see additional information on the Python program. There are some options that you can take advantage of once you learn all of the different commands.

C:\> python -h

Taking advantage of the filename feature will help you to designate which program Python opens when commanded. If you have a file labeled help.py, then all you need to do is open it after that type in Python, then the file name. This will make it much easier to open your files and work on them in the Python program. Be sure to keep a list of all the files you are working on to make finding them easy.

C:\> python help.py

C:\> python C:\Python27\Scripts\help.py

While "argument" sounds like something most of us have with our spouse from time to time, it means something entirely different in the world of Python. The word argument in Python-speak means a file that helps to alter what an application does. You need to remember that each of the characters used in Python is case sensitive. This means that the command" –t" is entirely different than "–T". Below are some of the most common commands and what they will do.

-d: By typing in this command, you will be able to initiate the Python debugger. The debugger tool will allow you to find errors in your program.

C:\> python -d help.py

-E: This option will allow you to ignore what are called environment variables. By doing this, you will be able to tweak your application to make it run better.

C:\> python -E help.py

-h: This option is needed when you are trying to find out more about the variables on the screen you are working on. You need to remember that Python will shut down immediately after this option

is performed, so save all work before going through with this command.

C:\> python -h help.py

-i: If you want to look at the code as you change it, this option will allow you to do just that.

C:\> python -i help.py

-m: This option will tell the program to stop processing and treat everything as one command in the system.

C:\> python -m help.py

-o: Using this option will help you to optimize the code you have written to make your application run faster.

C:\> python -o help.py

-OO: If you want to optimize further and remove docstrings, then this is the option you will need to use.

C:\> python -OO help.py

-q—Avoiding the printing of copyright and version can be prevented by using this interactive startup option.

C:\> python -q help.py

-s: This command will force the Python system to eliminate user directories.

C:\> python -s help.py

-*S*: Using this command may cause Python to neglect to find modules that it needs during the startup of an app.

C:\> python -S help.py

-*u*: This will help the unbuffered binary input to be on the standard output.

C:\> python -u help.py

-*v*: Verbose mode will allow you to read all of the critical statements about the application.

C:\> python -v help.py

-*V*: This will allow you to see the version number of the Python program before exiting.

C:\> python -V help.py

-*W*: If you want to change the warning level that the program displays, you will want to use this option.

C:\> python -W help.py

The more you can mess with these various commands, the easier you will find it to get an idea of what they do and how they can help you out. Here are some of the most common Python environment variables and what they do.

PYTHONCASEOK=x: This is a Windows-only variable that allows you to ignore case when parsing import statements.

PYTHONDEBUG=x: Using this option will initiate the debugging program.

PYTHONDONTWRITEBYTECODE=x: This will give you the same results as using the –B option.

PYTHONDEFAULTHANDLER=x: If you want to eliminate the list of calls that lead to an error, you will need to use this variable.

PYTHONHOME=arg: This will define the search path that Python uses to find modules.

PYTHONINSPECT=x: Using this variable will give you the same results as the –i option.

PYTHONIOENCODING=arg: This will specify encoding errors that are used in stdin or stderr devices.

PYTHONOPTIMIZE=arg: Using this variable will allow you to optimize the code that you have already written.

Typing the Commands

Once you have opened a command line in Python, you will be able to use some of the options and variables. The entire idea behind a command line is to allow you to issue commands and perform tasks with just a few lines of code. To tell the computer you are done with a particular command, you will need to hit the Enter key. Once you do this, you will be able to start a new command and move on to the next task.

After a while, you will begin to notice that you are remembering the steps of entering code without even looking at reference materials. Practice makes one perfect when it comes to using Python. Without diving into this type of programming head first, you will find it very hard to get a firm grasp on it. There are some helpful aspects to the Python programming that will allow you to get the help you need when you need it.

Now that you have learned some of the commands that you will use with the Python program, you are ready to know about developing an application.

Your First Python Program

Below is a snapshot of the Python interpreter, where we write the following command:

```
print("Hello World")
```

```
Command Prompt - python
C:\>python
Python 3.6.3 (v3.6.3:2c5fed8, Oct  3 2017, 17:26:49) [MSC v.1900 32 bit (Intel)] on win32
Type "help", "copyright", "credits" or "license" for more information.
>>> print("Hello World")
Hello World
>>>
```

The 'print' command is used to output text back to the console. In the remainder of this book, we will focus on writing programs that can encapsulate these code statements to build bigger and better programs in Python.

Creating a Python File

We start by creating a new file. We can either use an Integrated Development Environment or simply create a file in Notepad. We will do the latter, seeing as it's much easier as a beginner.

Let's look at the steps to create a simple Python program:

Create a new file in Notepad.

Add the following line of code inside the file.

```
print("Hello World")
```

Save the file as 'Demo.py'. Note that we are saving the file with the .py extension. This helps ensure that the Python runtime will be able to interpret the file and run it accordingly.

Running a Python File

Next, depending on the environment you are in, there are different ways to run the program. In Windows, we can carry out the following steps:

Open Windows PowerShell by using the Windows search feature.

In PowerShell, type the following command.

& python 'location of the file'

In the screenshot below, our Python code file is located on H drive.

```
Administrator: Windows PowerShell
Windows PowerShell
Copyright (C) Microsoft Corporation. All rights reserved.

PS C:\WINDOWS\system32> & python H:/Demo.py
Hello World
PS C:\WINDOWS\system32> _
```

When we hit enter, we get the relevant output, 'Hello World'. That's it!

What happens in the above process is that PowerShell submits our program to the Python interpreter, which then executes the program and returns the output back to the PowerShell console. This simple flow is depicted below.

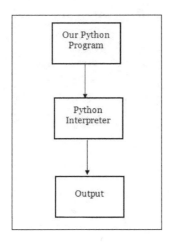

Now let's add a couple more lines of code to see how to execute multiple statements in Python.

Example 10: The following program is used to explore our first Python program further.

In our current program, let's add the following lines:

```
print("This is our first program")

print("We want to write to the console")

print("Hello World")
```

Note that unlike other programming languages, there is no main method or extra code needed to define the entry point for the program. It's just plain and simple code that gets executed.

From the output above, we can see that all the lines of code are executed, and the relevant text is written to the console.

The Python interpreter does the basic error checking for our Python programs. To illustrate how this works, let's make a mistake in our next program.

Example 11: The following program is used to introduce an error in the program.

Let's change our code to the following:

```
print{"This is our first program"}

print("We want to write to the console")

print("Hello World")
```

Note that we have changed the first line of code and used curly braces instead of the standard brackets. When we execute the program, we will get the following output: **PS H:\> & python H:/Demo.py**

File "H:/Demo.py", line 1

print{"This is our first program"}

^

SyntaxError: invalid syntax

Here we can see that the Python interpreter has checked the correctness of the program and pointed out the error accordingly.

Defining Values

We can also define values in a Python program. We will be looking at this in more detail in subsequent chapters, but for now, let's look at a simple example of how this can be done.

Example 12: The following program shows how we work with values in a program.

```
a="5"

print("The value of a is "+a)
```

This program's output will be as follows:

The value of a is 5

In the above program:

We first defined a variable called 'a'. We then assigned a value of '5' to this variable. We also use the 'print' statement to output the value of the variable. Note that in the print statement, we added the text 'The value of a is' before the actual value of the variable 'a'.

Using Python Libraries

Python has a host of built-in libraries that provide additional functionality to Python programs. We will be looking at this in greater detail later on, but for now, let's look at a simple example of how this works.

Example 13: The following program shows how to work with Python libraries.

```
print(sum([1,2,3]))
```

This program's output will be as follows:

6

In the above program:

We are making use of the math library. This is a built-in library that is always available.

We then use the 'sum' method in that library to carry out the multiplication of the numbers.

Lastly, we print the resultant value to the console.

We can also use other library modules that are not directly accessible. This is done by importing them. Let's look at an example of this.

Example 14: The following program illustrates how to import Python libraries.

```
import random

print(random.randint(1,5))
```

This program's output will depend on what gets generated. In our case, we received the following: **3**

In the above program:

We are first using the 'import' statement to get the functionality of the 'random' library.

We then use the 'randint' method to generate a random number between 1 and 5.

Lastly, we display that value to the console.

Using Comments

Comments are extremely useful in any programming language to ensure better readability and maintainability of the program. Their main purpose is to describe the various sections of the program for future reference. Let's look at the use of comments in Python.

Example 15: The following program shows how to use comments in a program.

```
# This program generates a random number

import random

print(random.randint(1,5))
```

In this sample program, the first line starts with a '#' which indicates that this is a comment line. As such, this line will not be executed and will be ignored by the interpreter.

CHAPTER 5:

PYTHON FOR DATA ANALYSIS

How Can Python Help with Data Analysis?

Now that we have had some time to discuss some of the benefits that come with the Python language and some of the parts that make up this coding language, it is now time for us to learn a few of the reasons why Python is the coding language to help out with all of the complexities and programs that we want to do with data science.

Looking back, we can see that Python has been pretty famous with data scientists for a long time. Although this language was not built to just specifically help out with data science, it is a language that has been accepted readily and implemented by data scientists for much of the work that they try to accomplish. Of course, we can imagine some of the apparent reasons why Python is one of the most popular programming languages, and why it works so well with data science, but some of the best benefits of using Python to help out with your data science model or project include:

Python is as simple as it gets. One of the best parts about learning how to work with the Python coding language is that even as someone who is entirely new to programming and who has never done any work in this in the past, you can grasp the basics of it pretty quickly. This language, in particular, had two main ideas in mind when it was first started, and these include readability and simplicity.

These features are pretty unique when we talk about coding languages, and they are often only going to apply to an object-oriented coding language and one that has a tremendous amount of potential for problem-solving.

What all of this means is that, if you are a beginner to working with data science and with working on the Python language, then adding these two together could be the key that you need to get started. They are both going to seem like simple processes when they work together, and yet you can get a ton done in a short amount of time. Even if you are more experienced with coding, you will find that Python data science is going to add a lot of depth to your resume and can help you get those projects done.

The next benefit is that Python is fast and attractive. Apart from being as simple as possible, the code that we can write with Python is going to be leaner and much better looking than others. For example, the Python code takes up one-third of the volume that we see with code in Java, and one-fifth of the volume of code in C++, just to do the same task.

The use of the common expressions in code writing, rather than going with variable declarations and space in place of ugly brackets, can also help the code in Python to look better. But, in addition to having the code look more attractive, it can help take some of the tediousness that comes in when learning a new coding language. This coding language can save a lot of time and is going to tax the brain of the data scientist a lot less, making working on some of the more complex tasks, like those of Data Analysis, much easier to handle overall.

The Python Data Analysis library, known as Pandas, is one of the best for helping us to handle all of the parts of not only our Data Analysis but also for the whole process of data science. Pandas can grab onto many data, without having to worry about lagging and other issues in the process. This is great news for the data scientist because it helps them to filter, sort, and quickly display their data.

Next on the list is that the Python library is quickly growing in demand. While the demand for professionals in the world of IT has seen a decline recently, at least compared to what it was in the past, the demand for programmers who can work with Python is steadily on the rise. This is good news for those who still want to work in this field and are looking for their niche or their way to stand out when getting a new job.

Since Python has so many great benefits and has been able to prove itself as a great language for many things, including programs for data analytics and machine learning algorithms, many companies who are centered on data are going to be into those with Python skills. If you already have a strong on Python, you can work to ride the market that is out there right now.

Finally, we come back to the idea of the vibrant community that is available with the Python language. There are times when you will work on a project, and things are just not working the way that you had thought they would, or the way you had planned. Getting frustrated is one option, but it is not going to help you to find the solution.

The good news with this is that you will be able to use the vibrant community, and all of the programmers who are in this community, to provide you with a helping hand when you get stuck. The community that is around Python has grown so big, and it includes members who are passionate and very active in these communities. For the newer programmer, this means that there is always an ample amount of material that is flowing on various websites, and one of these may have the solution that you are looking for when training your data.

Once you are able to get the data that you want to use and all of the libraries that work with as well, you can work on this community to see some of the results that you want. Never get stuck and just give up on a project or an idea that you have with your code, when you have that community of programmers and more, often many of whom have a lot of experience with Python, who will be able to help answer your questions and get that problem solved.

As we work through this guidebook, and you do more work with Python and Data Analysis, you will find that many libraries are compatible with Python that can help to get the work done. These are all going to handle different algorithms and different tasks that you want to get done during your Data Analysis, so the ones that you will want to bring out may vary. There are many great choices that you can make, including TensorFlow, Pandas, NumPy, SciPy, and ScikitLearn, to name a few. Sometimes these libraries work all on their own, and sometimes they need to be combined with another library so that they can draw features and functionalities from each other. When we can choose the right library to work with, and we learn how to make them into the model that we need, our Data Analysis is going to become more efficient overall. While there may be other programming languages out there that are able to handle the work of Data Analysis, and that may be able to help us create the models that we need to see accurate insights and predictions based on the data, none of them are going to work as well as the Python library. Taking the time to explore this library and seeing what it can do for your Data Analysis process can be a winner when it comes to your business and using data science to succeed.

How Does Python Fit into Data analysis?

The next thing on our list that we need to focus on is how we can work with Python in order to complete the data analysis that we would like. There are a lot of different parts that come with our data analysis, and having it all come together, is going to take us some time and some good planning in the process. At one point, though, we will need to go through and make sure that we are working with a programming language, one that is versatile and strong, and one that is going to help us to run our algorithms as we go.

Our algorithms are very important to how well the data analysis will work. These are the pars that will take ahold of our data, and look through it all, sorting it through and telling us the insights or the patterns that are inside of it. But to get these to work well and to make sure that we are not going to end up with a big mess in the end and inaccurate results, we need to make sure that we are choosing a good and a strong language to get it done.

There are a lot of different coding languages that we can work with, and each one is going to bring about its own positives and negatives that we need to deal with. If you hear about the idea of coding and learning how to do a programming language, and it makes you nervous and anxious, have no fear. There are a lot of different languages that we can focus on to help us to handle our algorithms and get the best results when we want to work with our data analysis.

The number one language that is going to work for data analysis, and the machine learning that we need to accomplish to handle these algorithms, is Python. As we are going to explore in this chapter, there are a lot of benefits that come with using Python, whether you just want to learn the basics of coding, or you are interested in handling something as complicated at data analysis. Let's dive in and see what some of these benefits are all about.

Python is an easy language to work with. If you are someone who has never done anything with coding before, and you are a bit nervous about getting started, and what that will be like, then the Python language is going to be one of the best options to help you get it off to a good start.

There are many options in coding languages out there, but a lot of them are going to be kind of difficult to learn. They are often reserved for some of the more complicated types of coding that you want to use, and you can build them later. But if you are a complete beginner in coding, then Python is going to be the best option for you.

Python has a large library that makes learning the codes easier. You will be amazed at how much power is going to be found when you work with Python, and how many options and functions are found in this language as well. Whether you are a beginner or looking to add a few other parts and coding languages to your skillset, you will find that the traditional Python library is going to have all of the parts that you need to be more successful with it.

There are a lot of extensions and other libraries that work with Python that are specifically designed to enhance its capabilities and make it work better for a good data analysis. Even though the traditional library that comes with Python is going to include a lot of the power and more that you want with coding, other extensions make sure you can complete some of the processes that you want with data science, data analysis, and even machine learning. Python, more than any other language, has a lot of these options, which can make it so much easier overall to get your work done.

There is a lot of power that you can enjoy when it is time to work on Python. Even though we have spent some time talking about how easy the Python language is going to be to learn, we have to remember that ease of use does not mean that you are missing out on power. The good news is that Python is going to come with a lot of power, and you will be able to use it to handle almost any project that you would like along the way.

The community of Python is going to be large, allowing even a beginner to get some of the assistance that they need along the way. This may not seem like a big deal, but when you are working on learning how to work with a new language, it is going to prove to be invaluable. Any time that you need to learn something new that you have a new question, or you get stuck, and you are not able to figure out how to get things fixed and to work again, that community is going to be the answer that you need.

The community is going to include programmers from all around the world. And often, they will have a lot of different experience levels when it comes to how much they know how to do with coding. As a beginner, you can easily join and be included. And many programmers are more advanced who are willing to share some of their time and knowledge with you as well. This helps to facilitate some of the work that you want to accomplish and can make it easier to learn something new.

You can use Python with some of the other languages that are sometimes a necessity when working with data analysis. For the most part, Python is going to work just fine with some of the work that you want to do with sorting, organizing, fixing, testing, training, and creating with data analysis. But there are a few algorithms that are going to perform a bit better when we work with some other coding languages.

The neat thing is that you can often use some of the libraries and extensions that come with Python to help fix this issue. You can write out the codes in the Python language, keeping it as easy and simple as possible. Then the extension is going to come in and take over, converting the language over to something else and then executing it all for you. It is as simple as that for you to continue using the Python language in the way that you would like and still get the work done that is necessary.

Python works really well when it comes to handling some machine learning, which is often the core component that we see with the algorithms that run data analysis. While the focus of this guidebook is more about the basics of Python and of data analysis, we will find that when it comes to working on the algorithms that we want to handle in all of this, they are going to be run through the use of machine learning.

Machine learning is simply a process that helps take a program or even a whole system and set it up so that it can run on its own. The programmer will not have to come in and figure out all of the ways the system should behave. The system will be able to take the information that it gathers, and what it learns from the user, and use that to become smarter and better at its job overall. It is the main technology that is going to help us to run our algorithms so we can learn the patterns and insights that are needed in data analysis.

And the main language that is used to help create some of these machine learning algorithms in Python. Python can be used for other parts of the data analysis process, but you will also find that it is useful for helping us to create, train, and test the algorithms, ensuring that they are going to behave properly as well.

As we can see, there are a lot of different benefits that you will be able to enjoy when it comes to using Python. You can enjoy Python whether you are looking to increase some of your own knowledge base of programming and more, or if you are just looking for something to add to your skill sets. But it also works well for things like machine learning and data analysis, which are all going to be combined together for many of the projects that we want.

There may be a few other languages out there that we can work with that can handle our algorithms and may have some extensions and libraries that work with them to get the work done. But none are going to be as easy to use, as efficient to work with or provide the benefits that we are looking for, as we can find with the Python language. If you are looking for something simple to work with and will provide you with all of the benefits of learning how to program without taking years or months to figure out, then Python is the right one to use.

CHAPTER 6:

DATA STRUCTURES

How Data is Structured

There are many different forms of data, but, at its highest level, data is mainly categorized in three ways:

- **Structured** – incredibly organized data, found in databases, CSV files (as values separated by commas,), or other repositories. The data format ensures it is right for computation and inquiries, using SQL or other structured languages.

- **Semi-structured** – data that doesn't follow the way data models are structured when associated with data tables like relational databases but does have markers and tags that keep the semantic elements apart and enforce hierarchy in the data fields and records.

- **Unstructured** – data that has no real structure, such as natural language text or audio streams.

Clearly, the most useful data is structured data because it is ready for immediate manipulation. As a rule, only around 20% of the total data is represented by structured data, while the remaining 80% is a combination of unstructured and semi-structured data.

Be aware, though; most of what we call unstructured data does have some kind of structure. Take an article for publishing on the internet, for example. While it is classed as unstructured, it does have a structure of sorts by way of tags and metadata for the article content. It is classed as unstructured because the content itself has no real structure that is usable straightaway.

There are two main types, mainly structured and unstructured, and the types of algorithms and models that we can run on them will depend on what kind of data we are working with. Both can be valuable, but it often depends on what we are trying to learn, and which one will serve us the best for the topic at hand. With that in mind, let's dive into some of the differences between structured and unstructured data and why each can be so important to our data analysis.

Structured Data

The first type of data that we will explore is known as structured data. This is often the kind that will be considered traditional data. This means that we will see it consisting mainly of lots of text files that are organized and have a lot of useful information. We can quickly glance through this information and see what kind of data is there, without having to look up more information, labeling it, or looking through videos to find what we want.

Structured data is going to be the kind that we can store inside one of the options for warehouses of data, and we can then pull it up any time that we want for analysis. Before the era of big data, and some of the emerging sources of data that we are regularly using now, structured data was the only option that most companies would use to make their business decisions.

Many companies still love to work with this structured data. The data is very organized and easy to read through, and it is easier to digest. This ensures that our analysis is going to be easier to go through with legacy solutions to data mining. To make this more specific, this structured data is going to be made up largely of some of the customer data that is the most basic and could provide us with some information including the contact information, address, names, geographical locations, and more of the customers.

In addition to all of this, a business may decide to collect some transactional data, and this would be a source of structured data as well. Some of the transactional data that the company could choose to work with would include financial information. Still, we must make sure that when this is used, it is stored appropriately, so it meets the standards of compliance for the industry.

There are several methods we can use to manage this structured data. For the most part, though, this type of data is going to be managed with legacy solutions of analytics because it is already well organized, and we do not need to go through and make adjustments and changes to the data at all. This can save a lot of time and hassle in the process and ensures that we are going to get the data that we want to work the way that we want.

Of course, even with some of the rapid rise that we see with new sources of data, companies are still going to work at dipping into the stores of structured data that they have. This helps them to produce higher quality insights, ones that are easier to gather and will not be as hard to look through the model for insights either. These insights are going to help the company learn some of the new ways that they can run their business.

While companies that are driven by data all over the world have been able to analyze this structured data for a long period, over many decades, they are just now starting to really take some of the new and emerging sources of data as seriously as they should. The good news with this one, though, is that it is creating a lot of new opportunities in their company and helping them to gain some of the momentum and success that they want.

Even with all of the benefits that come with structured data, this is often not the only source of data that companies are going to rely on. First off, finding this kind of data can take a lot of time and can be a waste if you need to get the results quickly and efficiently. Collecting structured data is something that takes some time, simply because it is so structured and organized.

Another issue that we need to watch out for when it comes to structured data is that it can be more expensive. It takes someone a lot of time to sort through and organize all of that data. And while it may make the model that we are working on more efficient than other forms, it can often be expensive to work with this kind of data. Companies need to balance their cost and benefit ratio here and determine if they want to use any structured data at all, and if they do, how much of this structured data they are going to add to their model.

Unstructured Data

The next option of data that we can look at is known as unstructured data. This kind of data is a bit different than what we talked about before, but it is really starting to grow in influence as companies are trying to find ways to leverage the new and emerging data sources. Some companies choose to work with just unstructured data on their own, and others choose to do some mixture of unstructured data and structured data. This provides them with some of the benefits of both and can really help them to get the answers they need to provide good customer service and other benefits to their business.

There are many sources where we can get these sources of data, but mainly they come from streaming data. This streaming data comes in from mobile applications, social media platforms, location services, and the Internet of Things. Since the diversity that is there among unstructured sources of data is so prevalent, and those businesses who choose to use unstructured data will likely rely on many different sources, businesses may find that it is harder to manage this data than it was with structured data.

Because of this trouble with managing the unstructured data, there are many times when a company will be challenged by this data in ways that they weren't in the past. And many times, they have to add in some creativity to handle the data and to make sure they are pulling out the relevant data, from all of those sources, for their analytics.

The growth and the maturation of things known as data lakes, and even the platform known as Hadoop, are going to be a direct result of the expanding collection of unstructured data. The traditional environments that were used with structured data are not going to cut it at this point, and they are not going to be a match when it comes to the unstructured data that most companies want to collect right now and analyze.

Because it is hard to handle the new sources and types of data, we can't use the same tools and techniques that we did in the past. Companies who want to work with unstructured data have to pour additional resources into various programs and human talent to handle the data and actually collect relevant insights and data from it.

The lack of any structure that is easily defined inside of this type of data can sometimes turn businesses away from this kind of data in the first place. But there really is a lot of potentials that are hidden in that data. We just need to learn the right methods to use to pull that data out. The unstructured data is certainly going to keep the data scientist busy overall because they can't just take the data and record it in a data table or a spreadsheet. But with the right tools and a specialized set of skills to work with, those who are trying to use this unstructured data to find the right insights, and are willing to make some investments in time and money, will find that it can be so worth it in the end.

Both of these types of data, the structured and the unstructured, are going to be so important when it comes to the success you see with your business. Sometimes our project just needs one or the other of these data types, and other times it needs a combination of both of them.

For a company to reach success, though, they need to be able to analyze, properly and effectively, all of their data, regardless of the type of the source. Given the experience that the enterprise has with data, it is not a big surprise that all of this buzz already surrounds data that comes from sources that may be seen as unstructured. And as new technologies begin to surface that can help enterprises of all sizes analyze their data in one place, it is more important than ever for us to learn what this kind of data is all about, and how to combine it with some of the more traditional forms of data, including structured data.

CHAPTER 7:

PANDAS

Pandas are built on NumPy, and they are meant to be used together. This makes it extremely easy to extract arrays from the data frames. Once these arrays are extracted, they can be turned into data frames themselves. Let's take a look at an example:

In: import pandas as pd

import numpy as np

marketing_filename = 'regression-datasets-marketing.csv'

marketing = pd.read_csv(marketing _filename, header=None)

In this phase, we are uploading data to a data frame. Next, we're going to use the "values" method to extract an array that is of the same type as those contained inside the data frame.

In: marketing_array = marketing.values

marketing_array.dtype

Out: dtype('float64')

We can see that we have a float type array. You can anticipate the type of the array by first using the "dtype" method. This will establish which types are being used by the specified data frame object. Do this before extracting the array. This is how this operation would look:

In: marketing.dtypes

Out: 0float64

1int64

2float64

3int64

4float64

5float64

6float64

7float64

8int64

9int64

10int64

11float64

12float64

13float64

dtype: object

Pandas are going to be a big name when we want to use the Python language to analyze the data we have, and it is actually one of the most used tools that we can bring out when it comes to data wrangling and data munging. Pandas are open-sourced, similar to what we see with some of the other libraries and extensions that are found in Python world. It is also free to use and will be able to handle all of the different parts of your data analysis.

There is a lot that you will enjoy when working with the Pandas library, but one of the neat things is that this library can take data, of almost any format that you would like, and then create a Python object out of it. This is known as a data frame and will have the rows and columns that you need to keep it organized. It is going to look similar to what we are used to seeing with an Excel sheet. When it is time to sort through our data and more, you will find that it is a lot easier to work with compared to some of the other options like loops or list comprehensions or even dictionaries.

There are a variety of tasks that we can do when it comes to working with the Pandas library, but we are just going to focus on a few of them to give you an idea of how we can work on this and make it behave in the manner that we want. To start with, we are going to use this library to help us to load and save our data. When you want to use this particular library to help out with data analysis, you will find that you can use it in three different manners. These include:

You can use it to convert a Python dictionary or list, or aa array in NumPy to a data frame with the help of this library.

You can use it to open up a local file with Pandas. This is usually going to be done in a CSV file, but it is also possible to do it in other options like a delimited text file or in Excel.

You can also open a remote file or a database like JSON or CSV on one of the websites through a URL, or you can use it to read out the information that is found on an SQL table or database.

There are going to be a few different commands that show up with each of these options. However, when you want to open up a file, you would want to use the code of:

Pd read_filetype()

It is also possible for us to go through and use Pandas to view and inspect some of our data. You do not want just to gather the data and call it good. You want to be able to look through the data and inspect it as well. Once you have had some time to load the data, then it is time to look at it and see what is inside of that set of data. This allows us to see how the data frame is going to look.

To start with this one, running the name of the data frame would give you a whole table, but you can also go through and look at just the first n rows of your choice or the final rows as well. TO make this happen, we would just need to work with the codes of df.head(n) or df.tail(n). Depending on the code that you decide to use, it is possible to go through and look through a lot of information and figure out what is inside of there, and what data is going to be the most important for that.

Some of the other commands that you will be able to use in order to get the most out of the Pandas library and to ensure that we are going to be able to view and inspect your data will include:

Df.mean(): This one is going to help us get back the means of all our columns.

Df.corr(): This one is going to give us back the correlation between the different columns that are found in a data frame.

Df.count(): This one is going to be helpful because it will give us back the number of values that are not considered null in each of the columns of the data frame.

Df.max(): This one is going to provide us with the highest value in each column.

Df.median(): This one is going to give us the median that we need in all of our columns.

Df.std(): This is a good one to use because it will provide us with the standard deviation that is found in all of the columns.

These are just a few of the different things that we can do when it comes to using the Pandas library. This is a good way to help us to get all of the different data analysis parts done safely and effectively. We can use it for all the different parts that come with data analysis, and if you combine it together with the arrays in NumPy, you can get some amazing results in the process.

Matrix Operations

This includes matrix calculations, such as matrix to matrix multiplication. Let's create a two-dimensional array.

This is a two-dimensional array of numbers from 0 to 24. Next, we will declare a vector of coefficients and a column that will stack the vector and its reverse. Here's what it would look like:

In: coefs = np.array([1., 0.5, 0.5, 0.5, 0.5])

coefs_matrix = np.column_stack((coefs,coefs[::-1]))

print (coefs_matrix)

Out:

[[1. 0.5]

[0.50.5]

[0.50.5]

[0.50.5]

[0.51.]]

Here's an example of multiplication between the array and the coefficient vectors:

In: np.dot(M,coefs_matrix)

Out: array([[5.,7.],

[20.,22.],

[35.,37.],

[50.,52.],

[65.,67.]])

In both of these multiplication operations, we used the "np.dot" function to achieve them. Next up, let's discuss slicing and indexing.

Slicing and Indexing

Indexing is great for viewing the nd-array by sending an instruction to visualize the slice of columns and rows or the index.

Let's start by creating a 10x10 array. It will initially be two-dimensional.

In: import numpy as np

M = np.arange(100, dtype=int).reshape(10,10)

Next let's extract the rows from 2 to 8, but only the ones that are evenly numbered.

In: M[2:9:2,:]

Out: array([[20, 21, 22, 23, 24, 25, 26, 27, 28, 29],

[40, 41, 42, 43, 44, 45, 46, 47, 48, 49],

[60, 61, 62, 63, 64, 65, 66, 67, 68, 69],

[80, 81, 82, 83, 84, 85, 86, 87, 88, 89]])

Now let's extract the column, but only the ones from index 5.

In: M[2:9:2,5:]

Out: array([[25, 26, 27, 28, 29],

[45, 46, 47, 48, 49],

[65, 66, 67, 68, 69],

[85, 86, 87, 88, 89]])

We successfully sliced the rows and the columns. But, what happens if we try a negative index? Doing so would reverse the array. Here's how our previous array would look when using a negative index.

In: M[2:9:2,5::-1]

Out: array([[25, 24, 23, 22, 21, 20],

[45, 44, 43, 42, 41, 40],

[65, 64, 63, 62, 61, 60],

[85, 84, 83, 82, 81, 80]])

However, keep in mind that this process is only a way of viewing the data. If you want to use these views further by creating new data, you cannot make any modifications to the original arrays. If you do, it can lead to some negative side effects. In that case, you want to use the "copy" method. This will create a copy of the array, which you can modify however you wish. Here's the code line for the copy method:

In: N = M[2:9:2,5:].copy()

Taking It Further with Pandas

The next option that we need to take a look at is a bit of the work that we can do with the Pandas library. This is one of the most important libraries that we can work with overall because it can handle pretty much all of the parts that come with data analysis. There isn't anything in data analysis that the Pandas library won't be able to help us out with.

Pandas are going to be one of the packages from Python that can provide us with numerous different tools to help us with data analysis. The package is going to come with a lot of different structures of data that can be used for the different tasks that we need to do to manipulate our data. It is also going to come with a lot of methods that we are able to invoke for the analysis, which is going to be really useful when we are ready to work on some of our machine learning and data science projects in this language. As we can imagine already, there are several benefits that we can enjoy when we work with the Pandas library, especially when compared to some of the other options out there. First, it is going to present for our data in a manner that is suitable to handle all of our analysis through the different data structures, in particular through the DataFrame and the Series structures. In addition to this, we are going to find that this is a package that is able to contain a lot of different methods that are going to be convenient for data filtering and more. The Pandas library will come with a lot of the utilities that we need to perform operations of Input and Output in a seamless manner. And no matter which format your data is going to come to us in, whether it is CSV, MS Excel, or TSV, the Pandas library is going to be able to handle it for us.

How to Install Pandas

When you work with the traditional Python distribution, you will find that it is not going to have the module of Pandas. You will need to go through the process of installing this to your computer in order to get it to work. The nice thing that you will quickly notice, though, is that Python is going to come with a tool that is known as pip, which is exactly what you want to use in order to install Pandas on your own computer. In order to do this specific installation, we need to go through and use the command below:

$ pip install pandas

If you already have the Anaconda program on your system, then you need to use a slightly different command to help you out. This command is going to be:

$ conda install pandas

It is often recommended that when you do this process, you go through and install the latest version of the Pandas package to get all of the new features and more that we need along the way. However, it is still possible to get some of the older versions, and you can install this one as well. You can just go through and specify which of the versions that you would like to use when working on the conda install code that we did above.

The Data Structures in Pandas

With some of this in mind, it is time for us to go through a few of the different things that we can do with the Pandas code. First, we need to look at the data structures. There are two of these data structures that we can work with, including the series and the DataFrame.

The first one here is the series. This is going to be similar to what we can work with when it comes to a one-dimensional array. It can go through and store data of any type. The values of a Pandas Series are going to be mutable, but you will find that the size of our series is going to be immutable, and we are not able to change them later.

The first element in this series is going to be given an index of 0. Then the last element that is going to be found in this kind of index is N-1 because N is going to be the total number of elements that we put into our series. To create one of our own Series in Pandas, we need to first go through the process of importing the package of Pandas through the insert command of Python. The code that we can use, including:

Import pandas as pd

Then we can go through and create one of our own Series. We are going to invoke the method of pd.Series() and then pass on the array. This is simple to work with. The code that we can use to help us work with this includes:

Series1 = pd.Series([1, 2, 3, 4])

We need to then work with the print statement to display the contents of the Series. You can see that when you run this one, you have two columns. The first one is going to be the first one with numbers starting from the index of 0 like we talked about before, and then the second one is going to be the different elements that we added to our series. The first column is going to denote the indexes for the elements.

However, you could end up with an error if you are working with the display Series. The major cause of this error is that the Pandas library is going to take some time to look for the amount of information that is displayed, this means that you need to provide the sys output information. You are also able to go through this with the help of a NumPy array like we talked about earlier. This is why we need to make sure that when we are working with the Pandas library, we also go through and install and use the NumPy library as well.

The second type of data structure that we are able to work with here will include the DataFrames. These are going to often come in as a table. It is going to be able to organize the data into columns and rows, which is going to turn it into a two-dimensional data structure. This means that we have the potential to have columns that are of a different type, and the size of the DataFrame that we want to work with will be mutable, and then it can be modified.

To help us to work with this and create one of our own, we need to either go through and start out a new one from scratch, or we are going to convert other data structures, like the arrays for NumPy into the DataFrame.

There are a lot of different parts that we are able to handle when it comes to the Pandas library. And getting this setup and ready to go for some of our own needs is important in this process as well. This is one of the best libraries to work with when it is time to handle our work with Python coding with data analysis. This can handle all of the different parts that come with the data analysis along the way.

CHAPTER 8:

NUMPY

N ow it is time for us to take a look at one of the great libraries that we can work with when it comes to using Python and getting our data analysis to work well for our needs. NumPy is one of the first that we can look at, and it is going to be one of the best. It is actually going to be the basis that we can see with some of the other important libraries that we will discuss later on, or other data analysis libraries, so it is worth our time to take a look at it.

To start with, NumPy is a library that is used in Python. We can use it for a number of different reasons, including numerical as well as scientific computing if we need it. For the most part, though, it is going to be used to help us compute our array s quickly and efficiently. We will have it based and written out in the Python and the C language.

Even though this is a language that works for the C language as well, this is going to be a basic data analysis library that we are going to use with Python, and the word NumPy is going to stand for Numerical Python. We are going to bring out this library to help us to process any of the homogeneous multidimensional arrays that we want to handle.

This library is going to be one of the core libraries that is used for different scientific computations. This means that it is going to have a powerful array of multidimensional objects, and it will integrate some tools that are useful when it is time to really work with these arrays as well.

You will quickly find that when you work with the data analysis that we have been talking about that NumPy is going to be useful in almost all of the scientific programming that we try to do with Python, including things like statistics, machine learning, and bioinformatics. It is also going to provide us with some good functionality that we can work with, functionality that is able to work well will run efficiently and is well written in the process.

Understanding More About NumPy

This library is really basic, but it is still going to be important when it comes to handling some of the scientific computing that we want to do with Python. Plus, it will not take that long working with data science and data analysis before you find that this is going to be the library that other data analysis libraries are going to be dependent on.

Some of the other major libraries are going to be dependent on the arrays in NumPy as their inputs and outputs. In addition to this, it is also going to provide some functions that are going to allow developers a way for developers to perform all of the basic and the advanced functions that they would like, whether we are talking about statistics or mathematics, especially when we are dealing with multidimensional arrays and matrices, without needing to use as many lines of codes to get it all done.

When we compare these arrays with the lists that we talked about earlier with Python, you will find that the arrays are going to be much faster. But Python lists do have an advantage over the arrays because they are more flexible as you are only able to store the same data type in each column when we are working with the arrays.

There are a few features that you are going to enjoy when it is time to work with the NumPy library. Some of the main features that you will enjoy the most will include:

The NumPy library is going to be a combination of Python and C language,

This is going to consist of arrays that are homogeneous and multidimensional. Ndarray is part of this as well, which will be n-dimensional arrays as well.

It is going to work on a lot of different functions for arrays if you would like.

It can also help us to reshape the arrays. It also allows Python to have a way to work as an alternative to MATLAB.

There are a lot of reasons why we would want to work with NumPy rather than having to pick one of the other libraries that are out there along the way. We will use the array in NumPy for the work that we are doing with Python instead of a list. And some of the reasons for this include it is convenient to work with, it is going to perform faster than other methods, and it is going to use less memory overall.

All of these are going to be important when we are trying to do some of the algorithms that we need in data analysis. And mostly, you will notice that the arrays are going to be the number one thing that we utilize when it is time to work with this library as well.

There are a few other things that we need to explore when it comes to how we are able to work with the NumPy library. First, the NumPy array is going to take up a lot less space than other options.

On the other hand, we are able to create an array, and it is only going to take about 4 MB. If you need to use a lot of different arrays as you go through, and they are going to fit better on the space of your memory overall. Arrays are also going to be easier to access when you would like to read and write on them later on.

In addition, the performance when it comes to speed, you will find that the NumPy arrays are going to be great. It is going to be able to perform a lot faster when it comes to computations than what we find with the Python lists. Because this library is considered open-sourced, it is not going to cost you anything to get started with. Then it also has the benefit of working with the popular Python programming language, which has high-quality libraries for almost all of the tasks that you want to accomplish.

All of these are great benefits to work with. You will find that it is a high-quality library that is going to help us to get things done. You can get it to match up with the libraries that you want, it is going to be free to work with, and it can handle a lot of the data analysis projects that you want to do. It is also an easy library that will connect some of the codes that are already existing in the C language over to the interpreter for Python so you can get your work done.

There are a lot of benefits that are going to come up when you want to work with the NumPy library, and you will find that it is going to be the basis for a lot of the codes and algorithms that you want to write out when you are working with your data analysis. Learning how to use this language and what it is able to do for you is going to make a world of difference in how much you are able to accomplish for the long-term, and it is worth your time to learn more about it as well to complete your project.

NumPy Package Installation

Earlier, we took some time to look at the different libraries that come with the Python language, and the ones that will work the best with data analysis. With that in mind, it is time for us to start working with some of the steps to installing the most basic, but also important, the library is known as NumPy.

We are going to install this on all three of the major operating systems to make it easier, and we will use the pip, which is the package installer for Python. This will make it easier to get things done and will ensure that the NumPy library is going to work on any computer that you would like. We can then talk about some of the basics of working with NumPy later on, so we see why this library is such an imprint one to work with.

Installing NumPy on a Mac OS

The first operating system that we will look at is how to install the NumPy on our Mac computers. We can do this with several different Python versions, and the steps are similar to one another to make things easier. To start, we need to open up the terminal on your computer. In addition, you get that open, type in python to get the prompt for this language to open for you. When you get to this part, follow the steps below to help get it going:

We want to press on Command and then the Space Bar. This will help us to open up the spotlight search. Type in the word "Terminal" before pressing on entering.

This should bring up the terminal that we want to use. We can then use the command of pip in order to install the NumPy package. This requires the coding of "pip install numpy" to get going.

Once you have gotten a successful install, you can type in python to this again to get that python prompt. You should check to see which version of python is displayed there. You can then choose to use your command of import in order to include the package of NumPy and use it in any codes that you would like in the future.

That method works the best with Python 2.7. You can also go through and install the NumPy package on Python 3. This is going to be similar. However, when you are done opening the terminal that we detailed in the first step above, you would use the pip3 command in order to install NumPy. Notice that we are going to work with pip3 rather than pip from before. Otherwise, the steps are going to be the same.

Installing NumPy on a Windows System

It is important to remember that the Python language is not going to be on the Windows operating system by default, so we need to go through and do the installation on our own to use it. You can go to www.python.org and find the version that you want to use. Follow the steps that are there in order to get Python ready to go on your own computer. Once you have been able to get Python installed successfully, you can then open up the command prompt that is on your computer and use pip in order to install the NumPy library.

Installing NumPy on the Ubuntu Operating Systems

Ubuntu and some of the Linux distributions may not be as common and as popular to work with as some of the other options out there, but they can still do many amazing things when it comes to helping us get our work done. It is a good option to use for things like hacking, machine learning, and data analysis, and it is known to work well with the Python language.

You will find that similar to the Mac operating system, Python is going to already be installed on this kind of computer. However, there is a problem because the pip is not going to be installed. If you would like to have the complete package to get this work done, download this from www.python.org, and then get it installed on your operating system using the apt install command to get this done.

In addition, there is an alternative manner to get this done. You can work with the install pip command on ubuntu and then install NumPy. This is often the better of the two ways to do it because it is simple and just needs a few commands. Keep in mind with this one that you have to have the root privileges on your system to help install pip and NumPy, or it will not work.

You can do all of this by opening up the terminal that is found in ubuntu and then install pip with the command of "pip3 using apt". Once you have this pip installed on your computer, you can then go through and install NumPy with the same commands that you used in the other operating systems.

Installing NumPy on Fedora

Another option that we are going to use is known as the Fedora operating system. This one is a bit different than we will see with some of the other options, but it does have a few of the steps that the Ubuntu system from before has. We are going to work with the pip command to help install the NumPy library.

Notice that there is going to be a difference in command of pip whether you are using it for Python 2.X or Python 3 and higher. This is specifically seen when we are working with the Fedora system. We will need to use pip install numpy to get the older version, but we will want to work with python3 -m pi install numpy for the newer versions.

It is easy to get both the Python language and the NumPy library installed in our computers, and no matter which operating system you decide to work with along the way, it is going to be an easy process to work with and get the library up and running. Once that is done, you can start to use this library directly, or use it as the main source to help some of the other libraries run and get to the arrays, which we will talk about in a bit.

Creating vectors and matrices from Python lists

Let us declare a Python list.

In []: # This is a list of integers

Int_list = [1,2,3,4,5]

Int_list

Out[]: [1,2,3,4,5]

Importing the NumPy package and creating an array of integers.

In []: # import syntax

import numpy as np

np.array(Int_list)

Out[]: array([1, 2, 3, 4, 5])

Notice the difference in the outputs? The second output indicates that we have created an array, and we can easily assign this array to a variable for future reference.

To confirm, we can check for the type.

In []: x = np.array(Int_list)

type(x)

Out[]: numpy.ndarray

We have created a vector, because it has one dimension (1 row). To check this, the 'ndim' method can be used.

In []: x.ndim # this shows how many dimensions the array has

Out[]: 1

Alternatively, the shape method can be used to see the arrangements.

In []: x.shape # this shows the shape

Out[]: (5,)

Python describes matrices as **(rows, columns)**. In this case, it describes a vector as **(number of elements)**.

To create a matrix from a Python list, we need to pass a nested list containing the elements we need. Remember, matrices are rectangular, and so each list in the nested list must have the same size.

In []: # This is a matrix

x = [1,2,3]

y = [4,5,6]

my_list = [y,x] # nested list

my_matrix = np.array(my_list) # creating the matrix

A = my_matrix.ndim

B = my_matrix.shape

Printing

print('Resulting matrix:\n\n',my_matrix,'\n\nDimensions:',A,

'\nshape (rows,columns):',B)

Out[]: Resulting matrix:

[[4 5 6]

[1 2 3]]

Dimensions: 2

shape (rows,columns): (2, 3)

Now, we have created a 2 by 3 matrix. Notice how the shape method displays the rows and columns of the matrix. To find the transpose of this matrix *i.e.* change the rows to columns, use the **transpose ()** method.

In []: # this finds the transpose of the matrix

t_matrix = my_matrix.transpose()

t_matrix

Out[]: array([[4, 1],

[5, 2],

[6, 3]])

Tip: Another way of knowing the number of dimensions of an array is by counting the square-brackets that opens and closes the array (immediately after the parenthesis). In the vector example, notice that the array was enclosed in single square brackets. In the two-dimensional array example, however, there are two brackets. Also, tuples can be used in place of lists for creating arrays.

There are other methods of creating arrays in Python, and they may be more intuitive than using lists in some applications. One quick method uses the **arange()** function.

Syntax: np.arange(start value, stop value, step size, dtype = 'type')

This method is similar to the **range()** method we used, for example, 43. In this case, we do not need to pass its output to the list function, our result is an array object of a data type specified by 'dtype'.

Example 56: Creating arrays with the arange() function.

We will create an array of numbers from 0 to 10, with an increment of 2 (even numbers).

In []: # Array of even numbers between 0 and 10

Even_array = np.arange(0,11,2)

Even_array

Out[]: array([0, 2, 4, 6, 8, 10])

Notice it behaves like the range () method form our list examples. It returned all even values between 0 and 11 (10 being the maximum). Here, we did not specify the types of the elements.

Tip: Recall, the range method returns value up to the 'stop value – 1'; hence, even if we change the 11 to 12, we would still get 10 as the maximum.

Since the elements are numeric, they can either be integers or floats. Integers are the default, however, to return the values as floats, we can also specify the numeric type.

In []: Even_array2 = np.arange(0,11,2, dtype='float')

Even_array2

Out[]: array([0., 2., 4., 6., 8., 10.])

Another handy function for creating arrays is **linspace()**. This returns a numeric array of linearly spaced values within an interval. It also allows for the specification of the required number of points, and it has the following syntax:

np.linspace(start value, end value, number of points)

At default, linspace returns an array of 50 evenly spaced points within the defined interval.

Example 57: Creating arrays of evenly spaced points with linspace()

In []: # Arrays of linearly spaced points

A = np.linspace(0,5,5) # 5 equal points between 0 & 5

B = np.linspace (51,100) # 50 equal points between 51 & 100

print ('Here are the arrays:\n')

A

B

Here are the arrays:

Out[ ]: array([0. , 1.25, 2.5 , 3.75, 5.])

Out[ ]: array([1., 2., 3., 4., 5., 6., 7., 8., 9., 10., 11., 12., 13., 14., 15., 16., 17., 18., 19., 20., 21., 22., 23., 24., 25., 26., 27., 28., 29., 30., 31., 32., 33., 34., 35., 36., 37., 38., 39., 40., 41., 42., 43., 44., 45., 46., 47., 48., 49., 50.])

Notice how the second use of linspace did not require a third argument. This is because we wanted 50 equally spaced values, which is the default. The 'dtype' can also be specified as we did with the range function.

Tip 1: Linspace arrays are particularly useful in plots. They can be used to create a time axis or any other required axis for producing well defined and scaled graphs.

Tip 2: The output format in the example above is not the default way for output in the Jupyter notebook. Jupyter displays the last result per cell, at default. To display multiple results (without having to use the print statement every-time), the output method can be changed using the following code.

In[]: # Allowing Jupyter output all results per cell.

run the following code in a Jupyter cell.

from IPython.core.interactiveshell import InteractiveShell

InteractiveShell.ast_node_interactivity = "all"

There are times when a programmer needs unique arrays like the identity matrix or a matrix of ones/zeros. NumPy provides a convenient way of creating these with the **zeros()**, **ones()** and **eye()** functions.

Example 58: creating arrays with unique elements.

Let us use the zeros () function to create a vector and a matrix.

In []: np.zeros(3) # A vector of 3 elements

np.zeros((2,3)) # A matrix of 6 elements *i.e.* 2 rows, 3 columns

Out[]: array([0., 0., 0.])

Out[]: array([[0., 0., 0.],

[0., 0., 0.]])

Notice how the second output is a two-dimensional array, *i.e.,* two square brackets (a matrix of 2 columns and 3 rows as specified in the code).

The same thing goes for creating a vector or matrix with all elements having a value of '1'.

In []: np.ones(3) # A vector of 3 elements

np.ones((2,3)) # A matrix of 6 elements *i.e.* 2 rows, 3 columns

Out[]: array([1., 1., 1.])

Out[]: array([[1., 1., 1.],

[1., 1., 1.]])

Also, notice how the code for creating the matrices requires the row and column instructions to be passed as a tuple. This is because the function accepts one input, so multiple inputs would need to be passed as tuples or lists in the required order (Tuples are recommended. Recall, they are faster to operate.).

In the case of the identity matrix, the function eye () only requires one value. Since identity matrices are always square, the value passed determines the number of rows and columns.

In []: np.eye(2) # A matrix of 4 elements 2 rows, 2 columns

np.eye(3) # 3 rows, 3 columns

Out[]: array([[1., 0.],

 [0., 1.]])

Out[]: array([[1., 0., 0.],

 [0., 1., 0.],

 [0., 0., 1.]])

NumPy also features random number generators. These can be used for creating arrays, as well as single values, depending on the required application. To access the random number generator, we call the library via **np.random**, and then choose the random method we prefer. We will consider three methods for generating random numbers: **rand()**, **randn()**, and **randint()**.

Generating arrays with random values.

Let us start with the rand () method. This generates random, uniformly distributed numbers between 0 and 1.

In []: np.random.rand (2) # A vector of 2 random values

np.random.rand (2,3) # A matrix of 6 random values

Out[]: array([0.01562571, 0.54649508])

Out[]: array([[0.22445055, 0.35909056, 0.53403529],

[0.70449515, 0.96560456, 0.79583743]])

Notice how each value within the arrays is between 0 & 1. You can try this on your own and observe the returned values. Since it is a random generation, these values may be different from yours. Also, in the case of the random number generators, the matrix specifications are not required to be passed as lists or tuples, as observed in the second line of code.

The randn () method generates random numbers from the standard normal or Gaussian distribution. You might want to brush up on some basics in statistics. However, this just implies that the values returned would have a tendency towards the mean (which is zero in this case), *i.e.,* the values would be centered around zero.

In []: np.random.randn (2) # A vector of 2 random values

np.random.randn (2,3) # A matrix of 6 random values

Out[]: array([0.73197866, -0.31538023])

Out[]: array([[-0.79848228, -0.7176693 , 0.74770505],

[-2.10234448, 0.10995745, -0.54636425]])

The randint() method generates random integers within a specified range or interval. Note that the higher range value is exclusive (i.e. has no chance of being randomly selected), while the lower value is inclusive (could be included in the random selection).

Syntax:_np.random(lower value, higher value, number of values, dtype)

If the number of values is not specified, Python just returns a single value within the defined range.

In []: np.random.randint (1,5) # A random value between 1 and 5

np.random.randint (1,100,6) # A vector of 6 random values

np.random.randint (1,100,(2,3)) # A matrix of 6 random values

Out[]: 4

Out[]: array([74, 42, 92, 10, 76, 43])

Out[]: array([[92, 9, 99],

[73, 36, 93]])

Tip: Notice how the size parameter for the third line was specified using a tuple. This is how to create a matrix of random integers using randint.

Illustrating randint().

Let us create a fun dice roll program using the randint() method. We would allow two dice, and the function will return an output based on the random values generated in the roll.

In []: # creating a dice roll game with randint()

Defining the function

def roll_dice():

""" This function displays a

dice roll value when called"""

dice1 = np.random.randint(1,7) # *This allows 6 to be inclusive*

dice2 = np.random.randint(1,7)

Display Condition.

if dice1 == dice2:

print('Roll: ',dice1,'&',dice2,'\ndoubles !')

if dice1 == 1:

print('snake eyes!\n')

else:

print('Roll: ',dice1,'&',dice2)

In []: # Calling the function

roll_dice()

Out[]: Roll: 1 & 1

doubles !

snake eyes!

Hint: Think of a fun and useful program to illustrate the use of these random number generators, and writing such programs will improve your chances of comprehension. Also, a quick review of statistics, especially measures of central tendency & dispersion/spread, will be useful in your data science journey.

Manipulating arrays

Now that we have learned how to declare arrays, we would be proceeding with some methods for modifying these arrays. First, we will consider the **reshape ()** method, which is used for changing the dimensions of an array.

Example 60: Using the reshape() method.

Let us declare a few arrays and call the reshape method to change their dimensions.

In []: freq = np.arange(10);values = np.random.randn(10)

 freq; values

Out[]: array([0, 1, 2, 3, 4, 5, 6, 7, 8, 9])

Out[]: array([1.33534821, 1.73863505, 0.1982571 , -0.47513784,
1.80118596,   -1.73710743,
 -0.24994721, 1.41695744, -0.28384007, 0.58446065])

Using the reshape method, we would make 'freq' and 'values' 2
dimensional.

In []: np.reshape(freq,(5,2))

Out[]: array([[0, 1],

[2, 3],

[4, 5],

[6, 7],

[8, 9]])

In []: np.reshape(values,(2,5))

Out[]: array([[1.33534821, 1.73863505, 0.1982571 , -0.47513784,
1.80118596],

[-1.73710743,   -0.24994721,   1.41695744,   -0.28384007,
0.58446065]])

Even though the values array still looks similar after reshaping, notice the two square brackets that indicate it has been changed to a matrix. The reshape method comes in handy when we need to do array operations, and our arrays are inconsistent in dimensions. It is also important to ensure the new size parameter passed to the reshape method does not differ from the number of elements in the original array. The idea is simple: when calling the reshape method, the product of the size parameters must equal the number of elements in the original array.

As seen in Example 60, the size parameter passed as a tuple to the reshape methods gives a value of 10 when multiplied, and this is also the number of elements in 'freq' and 'values' respectively.

There are times when we may need to find the maximum and minimum values within an array (or real-world data), and possibly the index of such maximum or minimum values. To get this information, we can use the **.max()**, **.min()**, **.argmax()** and **.argmin()** methods respectively.

Example 61:

Let us find the maximum and minimum values in the 'values' array, along with the index of the minimum and maximum within the array.

In []: A = values.max();B = values.min();

C = values.argmax()+1; D = values.argmin()+1

```
print('Maximum value: {}\nMinimum Value: {}\
```

```
\nItem {} is the maximum value, while item {}\
```

```
is the minimum value'.format(A,B,C,D))
```

Output

Maximum value: 1.8011859577930067

Minimum Value: -1.7371074259180737

Item 5 is the maximum value, while item 6 is the minimum value

A few things to note in the code above: The variables C&D, which defines the position of the maximum and minimum values are evaluated as shown [by adding 1 to the index of the maximum and minimum values obtained via **argmax ()** and **argmin ()**], because Python indexing starts at zero. Python would index maximum value at 4, and minimum at 5, which is not the actual positions of these elements within the array (you are less likely to start counting elements in a list from zero! Unless you are Python, of course.).

Another observation can be made in the code. The print statement is broken across a few lines using enter. To allow Python to know that the next line of code is a continuation, the backslash '\' is used. Another way would be to use three quotes for a multiline string.

Indexing and selecting arrays

Array indexing is very much similar to List indexing with the same techniques of item selection and slicing (using square brackets). The methods are even more similar when the array is a vector.

Example 62:

In []: # Indexing a vector array (values)

values

values[0] # grabbing 1st item

values[-1] # grabbing last item

values[1:3] # grabbing 2nd & 3rd item

values[3:8] # item 4 to 8

Out[]: array([1.33534821, 1.73863505, 0.1982571 , -0.47513784, 1.80118596, -1.73710743, -0.24994721, 1.41695744, -0.28384007, 0.58446065])

Out[]: 1.3353482110285562

Out[]: 0.5844606470172699

Out[]: array([1.73863505, 0.1982571])

Out[]: array([-0.47513784, 1.80118596, -1.73710743, -0.24994721, 1.41695744])

The main difference between arrays and lists is in the broadcast property of arrays. When a slice of a list is assigned to another variable, any changes on that new variable does not affect the original list. This is seen in the example below:

In []: num_list = list(range(11)) # *list from 0-10*

num_list # display list

list_slice = num_list[:4] # *first 4 items*

list_slice # display slice

list_slice[:] = [5,7,9,3] # *Re-assigning elements*

list_slice # display updated values

checking for changes

print(' The list changed !') if list_slice == num_list[:4]\

else print(' no changes in original list')

Out[]: [0, 1, 2, 3, 4, 5, 6, 7, 8, 9, 10]

Out[]: [0, 1, 2, 3]

Out[]: [5, 7, 9, 3]

no changes in the original list

For arrays, however, a change in the slice of an array also updates or broadcasts to the original array, thereby changing its values.

In []: # Checking the broadcast feature of arrays

num_array = np.arange(11) # *array from 0-10*

num_array # display array

array_slice = num_array[:4] # *first 4 items*

array_slice # display slice

array_slice[:] = [5,7,9,3] # *Re-assigning elements*

array_slice # display updated values

num_array

Out[]: array([0, 1, 2, 3, 4, 5, 6, 7, 8, 9, 10])

Out[]: array([0, 1, 2, 3])

Out[]: array([5, 7, 9, 3])

Out[]: array([5, 7, 9, 3, 4, 5, 6, 7, 8, 9, 10])

This happens because Python tries to save memory allocation by allowing slices of an array to be like shortcuts or links to the actual array. This way it doesn't have to allocate a separate memory location to it. This is especially ingenious in the case of large arrays whose slices can also take up significant memory. However, to take up a slice of an array without broadcast, you can create a 'slice of a copy' of the array. The **array.copy()** method is called to create a copy of the original array.

In []: # Here is an array allocation without broadcast

num_array # Array from the last example

copies the first 4 items of the array copy

array_slice = num_array.copy()[:4]

array_slice # display array

array_slice[:] = 10 # *re-assign array*

array_slice # display updated values

num_array # checking original list

Out[]: array([5, 7, 9, 3, 4, 5, 6, 7, 8, 9, 10])

Out[]: array([5, 7, 9, 3])

Out[]: array([10, 10, 10, 10])

Out[]: array([5, 7, 9, 3, 4, 5, 6, 7, 8, 9, 10])

Notice that the original array remains unchanged.

For two-dimensional arrays or matrices, the same indexing and slicing methods work. However, it is always easy to consider the first dimension as the rows and the other as the columns. To select any item or slice of items, the index of the rows and columns are specified. Let us illustrate this with a few examples:

Grabbing elements from a matrix

There are two methods for grabbing elements from a matrix: **array_name[row][col] or array_name[row,col].**

In []: # Creating the matrix

matrix = np.array(([5,10,15],[20,25,30],[35,40,45]))

matrix #display matrix

matrix[1] # Grabbing second row

matrix[2][0] # Grabbing 35

matrix[0:2] # Grabbing first 2 rows

matrix[2,2] # Grabbing 45

Out[]: array([[5, 10, 15],

 [20, 25, 30],

 [35, 40, 45]])

Out[]: array([20, 25, 30])

Out[]: 35

Out[]: array([[5, 10, 15],

 [20, 25, 30]])

Out[]: 45

Tip: It is recommended to use the **array_name[row,col]** method, as it saves typing and is more compact. This will be the convention for the rest of this section.

To grab columns, we specify a slice of the row and column. Let us try to grab the second column in the matrix and assign it to a variable column_slice.

In []: # Grabbing the second column

column_slice = matrix[:,1:2] # *Assigning to variable*

column_slice

Out[]: array([[10],

[25],

[40]])

Let us consider what happened here. To grab the column slice, we first specify the row before the comma. Since our column contains elements in all rows, we need all the rows to be included in our selection, hence the ':' sign for all. Alternatively, we could use '0:', which might be easier to understand. After selecting the row, we then choose the column by specifying a slice from '1:2', which tells Python to grab from the second item up to (but not including) the third item. Remember, Python indexing starts from zero.

Exercise: Try to create a larger array, and use these indexing techniques to grab certain elements from the array. For example, here is a larger array:

In []: # 5 × 10 Array of even numbers between 0 and 100.

large_array = np.arange(0,100,2).reshape(5,10)

large_array # *show*

Out[]: array([[0, 2, 4, 6, 8, 10, 12, 14, 16, 18],

[20, 22, 24, 26, 28, 30, 32, 34, 36, 38],

[40, 42, 44, 46, 48, 50, 52, 54, 56, 58],

[60, 62, 64, 66, 68, 70, 72, 74, 76, 78],

[80, 82, 84, 86, 88, 90, 92, 94, 96, 98]]])

Tip: Try grabbing single elements and rows from random arrays you create. After getting very familiar with this, try selecting columns. The point is to try as many combinations as possible to get you familiar with the approach.

If the slicing and indexing notations are confusing, try to revisit the section under list or string slicing and indexing.

Click this link to revisit the examples on slicing: List indexing

Conditional selection

Consider a case where we need to extract certain values from an array that meets a Boolean criterion. NumPy offers a convenient way of doing this without having to use loops.

Using conditional selection

Consider this array of odd numbers between 0 and 20. Assuming we need to grab elements above 11. We first have to create the conditional array that selects this:

In []: odd_array = np.arange(1,20,2) # *Vector of odd numbers*

odd_array # Show vector

bool_array = odd_array > 11 # *Boolean conditional array*

bool_array

Out[]: array([1, 3, 5, 7, 9, 11, 13, 15, 17, 19])

Out[]: array([False, False, False, False, False, False, True, True, True, True])

Notice how the bool_array evaluates to True at all instances where the elements of the odd_array meet the Boolean criterion.

The Boolean array itself is not usually so useful. To return the values that we need, we will pass the Boolean_array into the original array to get our results.

In []: useful_Array = odd_array[bool_array] # *The values we want*

useful_Array

Out[]: array([13, 15, 17, 19])

Now, that is how to grab elements using conditional selection. There is, however, a more compact way of doing this. It is the same idea, but it reduces typing.

Instead of first declaring a Boolean_array to hold our true values, we just pass the condition into the array itself, as we did for useful_array.

In []: # This code is more compact

compact = odd_array[odd_array>11] # *One line*

compact

Out[]: array([13, 15, 17, 19])

See how we achieved the same result with just two lines? It is recommended to use this second method, as it saves coding time and resources.

The first method helps explain how it all works.

However, we would be using the second method for all other instances in this book.

Exercise: The conditional selection works on all arrays (vectors and matrices alike). Create a two 3 $\times$ 3 array of elements greater than 80 from the 'large_array' given in the last exercise.

Hint: use the reshape method to convert the resulting array into a 3 $\times$ 3 matrix.

CHAPTER 9:

DATA ANALYSIS TIPS AND TRICKS

Understand the business before starting to solve any problems

W hile the data scientist may be excited to get started, you have to understand what you are looking for before you can do the work.

Otherwise, you may use the wrong method or algorithm, or you are going to just end up with a lot of information that looks like a mess. It is best to understand the business before you take up the project.

If you already work for that company and you do this in-house, then it shouldn't be an issue.

Some of the things that you should explore the business to help you out include:

- **Customer level information***:* You need to have some ideas about the customers the company has. This could be a month on month customer attrition, several active customers, and more.

- **Business strategies**: This would be a look at the way that the company gets new customers and how they work to keep their valuable customers.

- **Product information**: You also need to have some information on the product or services that the company offers. You can ask how the customer will interact with the products and how they earn money through the product. Learn as much about the product as possible before starting.

If you can go through and answer these questions, then you have a good start to working on the project.

Figure out the right evaluation method you should use

This is not meant to be a difficult puzzle to solve for you as an analyst, but this is also a trap that some will find themselves in.

Let's say that you are doing the data analysis to come up with a targeting model for a new marketing campaign. You need to know which model you are going to use to get the right information out of your data set.

The best way to figure this out is to take a look at the information that you have and figure out which method would be the best for you. Some types of data are going to lend themselves better to one method over another, and you will see this pretty quickly. Other times, you may have to try a few of the methods to see which one gives you the best results, or at least the results that look the least confusing.

Break out of the industry silos to get alternate solutions

Analytics is being used in almost all business industries. So instead of staying in traditional approaches, that are found with your particular business, why not go beyond that and see if other industries have found the solution that you are looking for.

A good example of this is a recommended video solution that was implemented in the e-commerce industry and can be used when you are doing a blogging portal. However, the only way that you are going to get this done is to interact with those who are working in the other industry. This can help you to learn how to make it happen and learn from them.

If you just sit there in your own industry and try to get things done, you may see some success, but you are missing out on some great opportunities. Our world is changing quickly, and many industries are using the same technology in different ways. Learning how some of these industries use data analysis can end up helping your own business, even if they are not really related.

Engage with your business counterparts

You should not be doing the whole analysis on your own. This will make you miss out on many important things. You must interact with other business partners and discuss what they are looking for, some of the important things about their business, and so on. As you go through the process, you should make sure that you keep in touch with them.

Sometimes this is hard. When you do the analysis for a business, they often want to stay away from the technical details because they are worried that these details would be too complicated. They would be just happy to receive the results at the end and then go through them and make decisions. However, if you want to do the best analysis possible, you must have a constant stream of interaction between you and the people you do the work for. This helps you to stay on track through it, find the right information, and even find some patterns that you may miss out on if you do the whole project on your own.

Keep the language simple

You do not need to dumb down the information so that it is watered out, but some statisticians like to use complex formulations that those people outside of the field cannot understand. Moreover, this is even easier to do when you work with data science. However, what you need to do is look at the output of variables that you have and then try to find a simple way to help the business understand what you are presenting to them.

Follow up on the chosen implementation plan

board with what you are doing and that they are being presented with the most up-to-date information possible. They will not want to receive the information just once and then call that good forever. The world of business is changing so fast that information they find valuable today may not count in a few weeks or months. A constant flow of new data will come in, and setting up meetings with the business and those in charge regularly will make it easier to ensure that they get the best and newest information to make important business decisions.

Read about the industry

The industry is always changing and growing. While something may have been difficult to do in the past, in a few months, it may be really easy because a new technique has developed.

You can learn from others in the field and even rely on some of the other industries which use this science to provide you with the solutions that you need.

Find new ways to improve

The field of data analysis is growing by leaps and bounds. It is a relatively new field, but it is really helping many businesses to grow and do well.

The only issue is that since it is so new, it is growing so quickly, and you will find that many new techniques and even new methods are going to come out in the future.

These can really improve what you can do in data science, but it means that you will always need to update your skills along the way.

Do not make the decisions for the company

Unless you are one of the managers in the company who has started doing data science, you do not get to make decisions for the company, and you do not get to push what ideas you think would be the best. Your job is to provide information for the company efficiently and quickly. You will, of course, write a report on the information that you find, and in a way that those in charge of decision-making can read through and see what the best course of action is. But you must only write down what is actually there, without any swaying or changing of the information and without giving your opinion.

CONCLUSION

Thank you for making it through to the end! The next step is to start putting the information and examples that we talked about in this guidebook to good use. There is a lot of information inside all that data that we have been collecting for some time now. But all of that data is worthless if we are not able to analyze it and find out what predictions and insights are in there. This is part of what the process of data science is all about, and when it is combined together with the Python language, we are going to see some amazing results in the process as well.

Many parts come with our data analysis, and we are going to spend some time talking about many of them inside of this guidebook. And we will look at how we can do it with the help of the Python coding language. When we can bring together the efficiency and the amazing features of data analysis with the ease of use and power that comes with the Python language, you will find that it is so good for your business and helping you to make some smart decisions along the way.

There are so many things that we need to work to get the successful data analysis that we have hoped for. It is a process that takes some good time, and you have to have the dedication and time to get it all done. However, this guidebook will show us the right steps to make that happen as quickly and efficiently as possible.

The staffing required for the data analysis will keep on expanding, and people from scientists to analysts to architects to the experts in the field of data management will be needed. However, a crunch in the availability of big data talent might see the large companies develop new tactics. Some large institutes predict that various organizations will use internal training to get their issues resolved. A business model having big data in the form of service can be seen on the horizon.

When you are ready to learn more about what data analysis can do for you, and how you can work with this data analysis to get the best results, along with the Python language, then it is time to take a look at what this guidebook has to offer!

More and more tools will become available for Data Analysis, and some of them will not need the analyst. Microsoft and Salesforce have announced some combined features, which will allow the non-coders to create apps for viewing the business data.

www.ingramcontent.com/pod-product-compliance
Lightning Source LLC
LaVergne TN
LVHW051247050326
832903LV00028B/2628